SNEAKER SEEKER

Featuring a big variety of the most exclusive and popular sneakers in the world this is the ultimate sneaker coloring book! Work on your fashion skills and create new editions of the legendary and popular sneaker designs.

EDITION NAME: _____
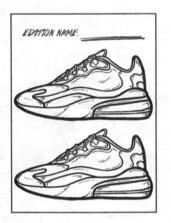

EDITION NAME: _____
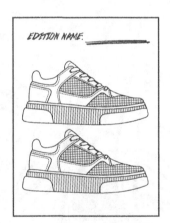

EDITION NAME: _____
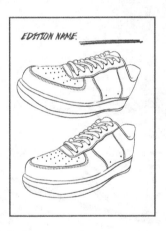

EDITION NAME: _____

EDITION NAME: _____

EDITION NAME: _____
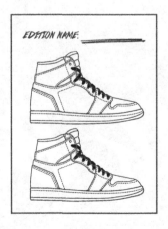

EDITION NAME: _____

EDITION NAME: _____

SNEAKERS

COLORING BOOK

COLOR TEST

SNEAKERS

COLORING BOOK

EDITION NAME:

SNEAKERS

COLORING BOOK

SNEAKERS

COLORING BOOK

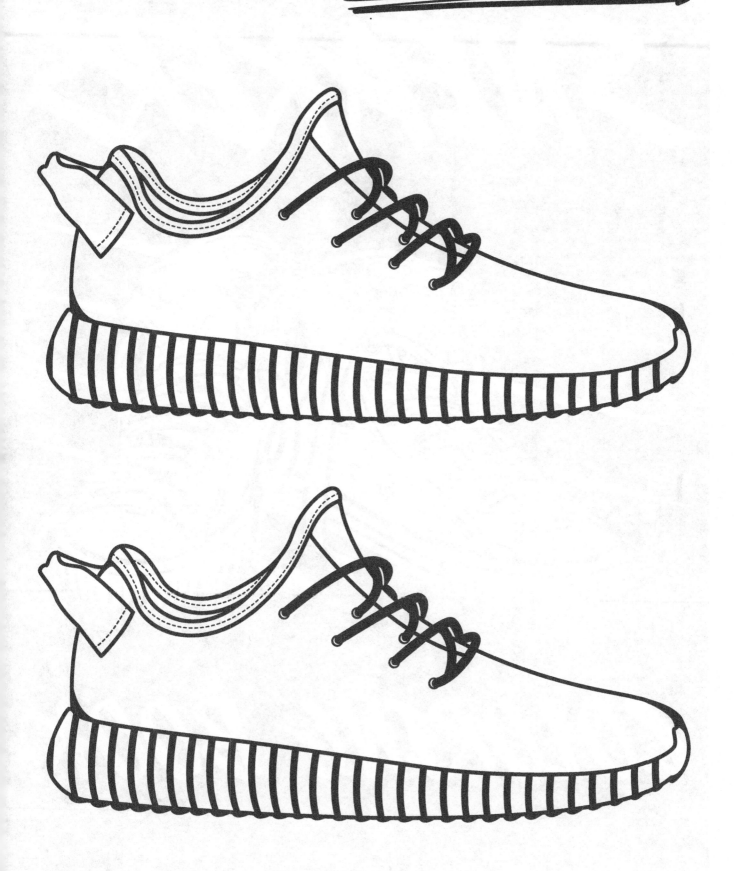

SNEAKERS

COLORING BOOK

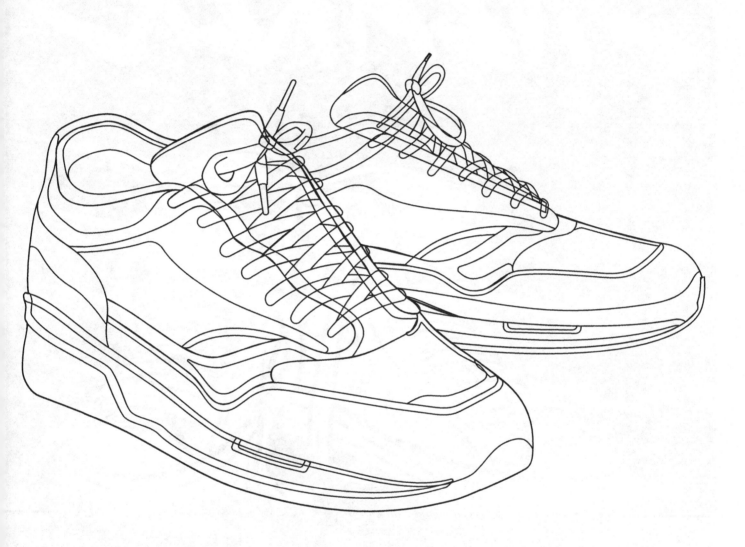

SNEAKERS

COLORING BOOK

EDITION NAME: _____

SNEAKERS

COLORING BOOK

EDITION NAME: _____

SNEAKERS

COLORING BOOK

EDITION NAME:

EDITION NAME:

EDITION NAME:

EDITION NAME:

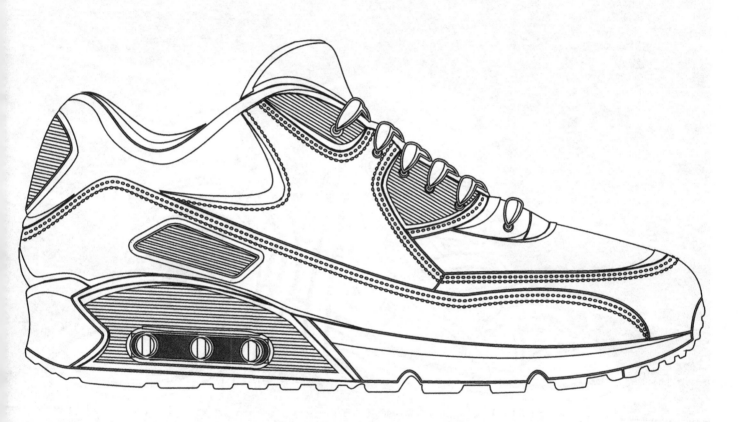

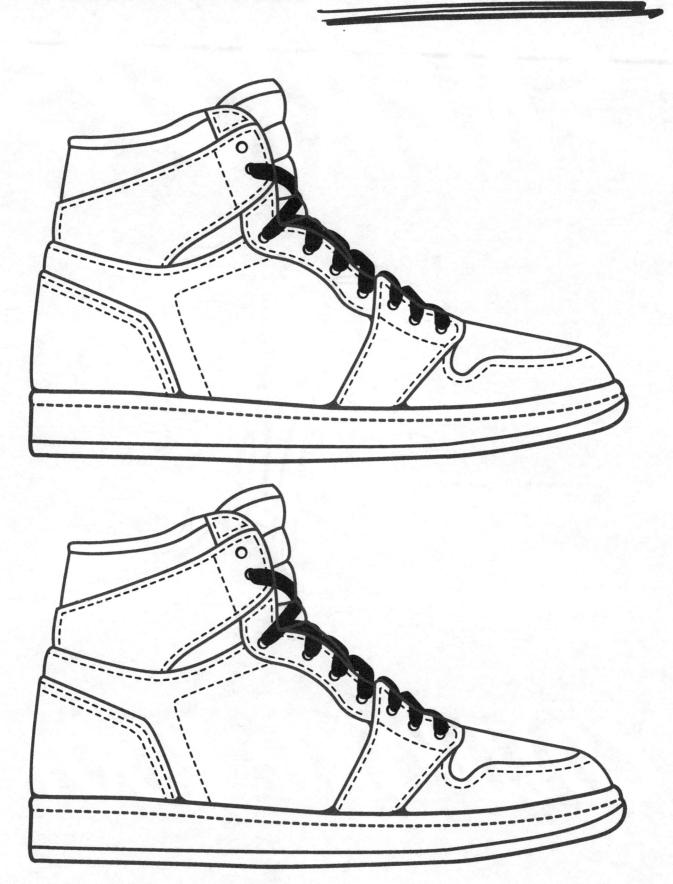

SNEAKERS

COLORING BOOK

SNEAKERS

COLORING BOOK

SNEAKERS

COLORING BOOK

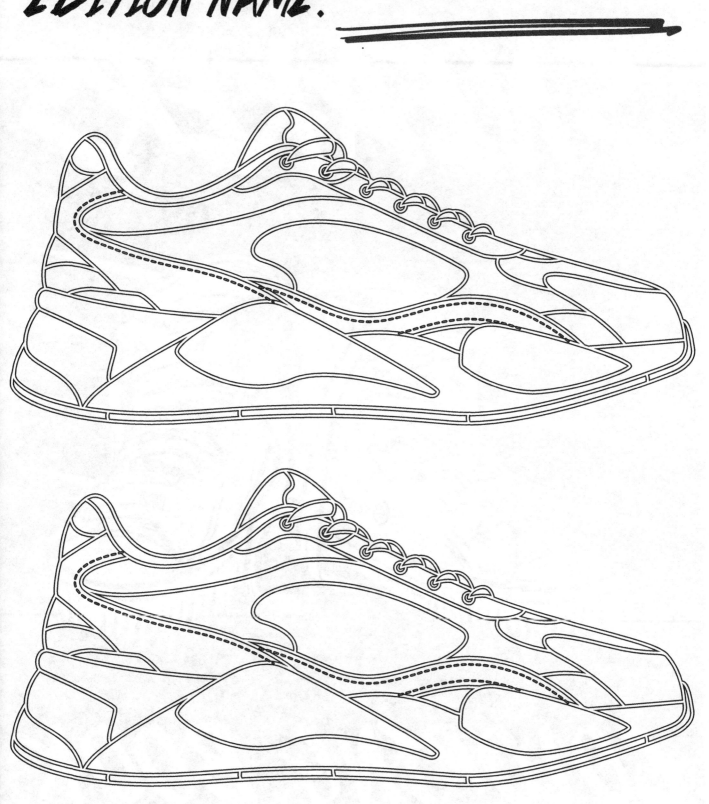

SNEAKERS

COLORING BOOK

SNEAKERS

COLORING BOOK

EDITION NAME:

EDITION NAME:

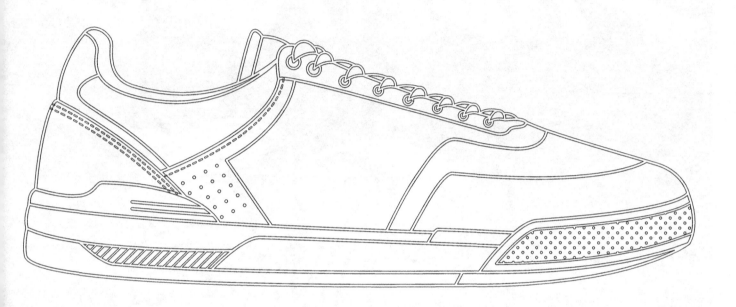

SNEAKERS

COLORING BOOK

SNEAKERS

COLORING BOOK

EDITION NAME:

SNEAKERS

COLORING BOOK

SNEAKERS

COLORING BOOK

SNEAKERS

COLORING BOOK

SNEAKERS

COLORING BOOK

EDITION NAME:

EDITION NAME:

SNEAKERS

COLORING BOOK

SNEAKERS

COLORING BOOK

EDITION NAME:

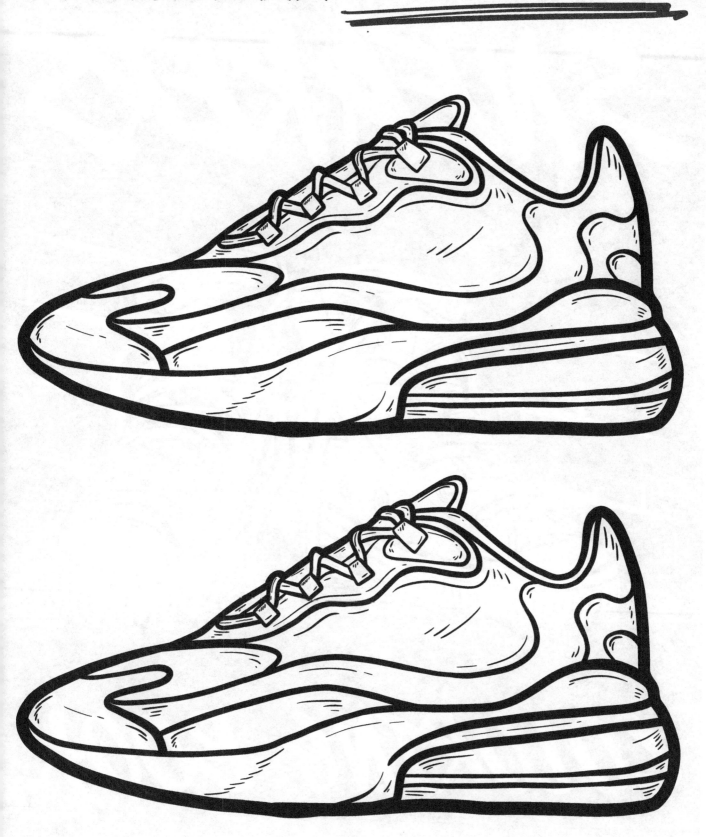

SNEAKERS

COLORING BOOK

SNEAKERS

COLORING BOOK

SNEAKERS

COLORING BOOK

Made in the USA
Monee, IL
25 October 2022

16525205R00044